Self-Portrait in a Convex Mirror 2

©2016 Paul Legault
All rights reserved

Book design by Joseph Kaplan
Cover Photography by Rachel Stern
Printed by McNaughton and Gunn

Published in the United States by Fence Books
Science Library, 320
University at Albany
1400 Washington Avenue, Albany, NY 12222

www.fenceportal.org

Distributed by Small Press Distribution
and Consortium Book Sales and Distribution.

Legault, Paul (1985–)

Publisher's Cataloguing-in-Publication data
Self-Portrait in a Convex Mirror 2 / by Paul Legault.
ISBN 13: 978-1934200933
Library of Congress Control Number: 2016933759

Fence Books are published in partnership with
the University at Albany and the New York State
Writers Institute, and with invaluable support
from the New York State Council on the Arts and
the National Endowment for the Arts.

Self-Portrait in a Convex Mirror 2
Paul Legault

Introduction

Self-Portrait in a Convex Mirror received the National Book Critics Circle Award, the National Book Award, and the Pulitzer Prize for poetry in 1975. (That's a pretty clean sweep.)

John Ashbery is the only living poet to have had the Library of America print vol. 1 of his Collected Work. That puts him in the company of Gwendolyn Brooks, Hart Crane, Gertrude Stein, William Carlos Williams, Louis Zukofsky, &c.

As a poet, and especially as a queer poet based in New York, his influence seems inescapable. The only way to get past it was to go through it. I never fully understood the ways in which I wrote like him, until I wrote like him on purpose.

Self-Portrait in a Convex Mirror 2 is a memory translation. I wrote down each of Ashbery's original poems, from memory. It is a reflection of *Self-Portrait in a Convex Mirror*'s reflection on Parmigianino's painting of his reflection in a convex mirror.

I remember. It goes like this:

"I don't find any direct statements in life. My poetry imitates or reproduces the way knowledge or awareness come to me, which is by fits and starts and by indirection. I don't think poetry arranged in neat patterns would reflect that situation. My poetry is disjunct, but then so is life."

—John Ashbery

"Repetition is the father of learning. I repeat. Repetition is the father of learning. Intelligence, all that, comes from repetition. Awareness, preparation, all that comes from repetition."

—Dwayne Michael Carter, Jr.

Table of Contents

Table of Contents

Self-Portrait in a Convex Mirror 2

I tried the immortal thing—part of it was free.
Somewhere else, we're somewhere where we are
Filtered into light by the thinnest layer of glass,
Waiting for ourselves to return. Words can be mean
or meaningless. Green yellows in the maple trees…

So this is about everything, obscurely enough.
I feel these invisible winds starting to move again
In this pile of pages ripped from some catalogue.
The new seconds second every motion. Summer
Will be here for most of the summer again,
Half-full with fullness, half-emptied of itself
At the mid-point you can't wander away from.
The more bored you are, the more you listen in
To what's prepared to be about to happen.

A look of glass stops you
As you walk past: am I the seen thing
In the car-window? Is it really me
Who wandered through this door into representation?
What I thought was the original I have had to grow
Into this combination of processes of thought
Used to determine, subjectively, how everything
Isn't myself per se: just sort of. In the morning,
Meanwhile, everywhere, the children of the afternoon
Sleep in. The Sun determines this moment to be

Dawn and it its own sphinx, wishing one thing
After the next. There will be more rides through
The hay over the laplands. The new sentences
Wetten this book as some high-priestess recites
The thing about the will of a people let out only
To sound their complicated network of horns.
I thought I could almost hear my shadow here.
It was actually just you telling me to come back,
Sweetly—rewritten as the speech stillness makes

To everything. The night is as shiny as the moon
Which decided to move again—into Heaven.
All the small things of the Earth make a sound.
The business of time is experiencing a boom.
Our reservations are confirmed for the afterparty.
Steal the book, burn its contents, read it back to me
From memory. The sky that's cast over the whole world
Is flat underground. This second version of the idea
Means more to you, reticently, than was perceived again.

Like the way rain gets wet, he said, in its own storm,
The idea of color gets braided into this texture
Of thought, and the place had known it was
Only a matter of time until the target went ahead
And flew westward, or up, or off, or else just
Wherever it was to be shot at in the rural festival.
I keep seeing things in the carpet. Clouds are not
An abstraction or two of them. One is a succotash.
One bothers the nurse nearly constantly
To remove the flaneur from his post
And the monitor from your now-quite-rested body.
One part had been separated all of a sudden,
And the chef offered it to you. A hand can be
Thought of fondly, even if it continues to elude you
In the coat room. They stained their white laundry white
Before entering the modern infrastructure
Where they go every day despite an untenable preference
For race-tracks built in the desert, staying in
And up until the late hours make their bird-noises
Through the paper wall, everything left out returned
And ready to be re-programmed. Surely they'd already written,
But the telephone was invented for a reason, that being
To speak low.
      Some man said, "You should be on the alert.
There are important events occurring
To everyone that should include you

If you are a self-respecting citizen."
I am at a loss, and that allows me
To have not thought of the thing all at once
Like a convertible in the rain. They make clocks
In America that look at you. Fire still exists
Though it's an obsolete technology. Prometheus
Is lost as a used lighter. Death's
A film I accidentally saw twice.

It was the shadow of something Venetian and borrowed
That made you notice the interior platform, cranked up
From the center of the floor with a woman on top
Reading, earnestly. It's not that the lighting was so bad
But that they released us at the exact moment lightning
Struck. White people tend to sidle off, eating wafers
On a sand-bar or crackers on the porch, or worse—
It always got that way—the background vegetables.

What was the big deal anyway?
His disguise was the black hole from which he emerged:
Volcanic, somewhat trivial, plagued by vision.
The gardenia laid out its dominion past reason,
And they allowed it. There should be no resistance. Two things
Knotted underwater like pilgrims to a tree. This type of magic's
Magic when magic's sad but chic. I've gotten used to it.
They've gone and presented the mind at rest
Inside of a body in a position previously described
In the plot summary. Things became too real. It was something
That happened to you. The circumstances were attenuated.
You can appreciate how the actuality differs in response
From its primary nature, darkly, on a stoop.

As You Came From The Holy Land 2

in parts of New York there's this state
of being lit as a bush with god or the future
what was driving that old panic into the air again
what's not classic about being something old
when did the magic lantern evolve into TV
we had been thinking of time in the miniature
as something worth avoiding at all costs
and the accountant stopped his installments
from reaching the interior immediately
in the habit of one born of an impetus
the silk worms abandoned their turrets
and that was that after all the hubbub
over the retraction of life from its leaving off
of what it was there in the estuaries

you stopped reading accurately so
things could change in the good way
from the old days still settling
what were the valid reasons to open up shop
when did you come for them in the Holy Land
with what provisions into the dear country
what did it all lead to by way of repetition
when did the solid masses rise up
you were admittedly a veteran to the experience
and before they took the census
they had counted you

Self-Portrait in a Convex Mirror 2

as one of them who watched us
the birds occurring to their hidden branch
the single light desiring its passage
into the horticultural night
we made an art of this enough
to manage the beautiful care
with which it all stopped
suddenly out of an impulse
in a round like a sign for trees
as pocketable as a cone
we had a home for it and one
we stitched to the current

a certain quality of distinction
with its new adages set into
what is right today before it turns left
the gap finding its own emptiness
striking before all creates a bell
and rustles toward the door
we had known inside of a brain
the weight breaking where it piles
time having past in an idea
and time having a new past

A Man of Words 2

No one particularly envied the position
Despite growing slightly suspicious
Of the nature he leant to his job
Which he did with some fervor.
The nettle exists to prosper in a field
That remains slightly olde.
The culture surrendered its authority
In front of its grown-up children, and we were wrong
To suggest a role could have anything
To do with the elements in their official state
Where everything gathers, for now.
Whether he would carry the torch having eaten
Apples or having laid them aside at the beach house
Did not affect who we began to expect there.
The evidence was overplayed.

Those truths lay unencumbered in their canopy
And the new outlook remained being what you saw there
When looking in that direction twice or thinking
Of a sound you made once at the threshold
Having noticed something was there that absconded.
The origin has this tendency to begin again.
Tell me about it or parse the subject after
Suggesting these concepts become our systems of us.
We behaved well enough on the team established
To be our discoverers of the internal world.
One idea behind the whole thing
Collapsed and one just shook a little.

Self-Portrait in a Convex Mirror 2

Into the enigmatic landscape
The aquatic world grew to be
Of a mission of thought, the catch-all being
Always that we go on beside us—thorough,
Noting the features where they've collected,
Suggestive of a time that counts twice.
She would never inquire into the matter on purpose
When what was made was to be taken out,
Removed of its former categorical impulse,
Its designs and how they landed
Upon a particle layer if one destined
To be nothing so daring as the earth
Nor as precious, nor as precious in a bad way.
Things continued to present themselves; things
Beheld their bright avenue, endlessly
And right away. The occurrence made its approach.
It will tell us about it. She will get on with it
For once. There is something rude about
The suddenness of the seagull's invitation
When morning could have just been and been
Again just that but to itself.
Within the new portraiture we met
Ourselves to form a rising ball
If only to create these dispersions
Of sight, everything adjusting to dusk's
Stingy allowance. The curtains contain

The implication of light. Talismans exchange
Their meaning for this largeness. We drive
Each other, our private engines
Stowed into the back of what the forest calls
The forest's garage. I went on about magic
Until a gun turned into a bird that turned
To the left over a plain by tipping its wing.
Then the plain turned into a mountain.

So they shifted at least one of the measurements
They had put to use in making the nets
And buried the catch altogether. Conversation
Proved to be a productive form of living inside
Without the constant interruptions of a hunt.
The grandparents beget their little champions
And what gets emitted emits
From a recognizable place they called the source
Of what mothers all the animals. You're put out.
Heaven develops its heaven-structure. You look like
A chancellor at the door to ripeness.
These trees balance a sort of jungle
Only to drop it when the days become
The good days and you our rationale
In the next ones. Now I'm in the proper boat.
The water symbols aren't all used up
In this ribald season. I moved into a shell.

Self-Portrait in a Convex Mirror 2

I still don't remember the storyline despite
The bells they tied to its hypothetical feet
Elongated in the Greek fashion
Of a flying messenger
Of a god put to work with little instruction
But nonetheless making good on what promised
To be an update to our likeness
Which is our likeness in an embrace,
In soft lighting, perpetually. The dynasty
Is offering a reward to these spaces
Of import cornered by the audience
They would be to the future of themselves. Dreams
Have trumped the process of having a party
At night or inside of another event
That has already gone, went, and begun
To happen to us in this sudden dome.
Everything's been restored. The math is all
Wrong. What would this dynasty become
If not an audience to the audience's power.
The act was its first attempt. The precedent
Balances the event. I cannot say why here,
But there's a place where someone is.

_____

Absolute Clearance 2

"Radical thinking is like not thinking about it too much…"
−Baudrillard

He drew a picture on the wall
Of the truth system,
One-part entirety, one-part dedicated
To the incremental changes in the room.

In the motel or camper or room
We granted passage from
The inner circles that led back, as they do,

To more nights out on the ocean.
The idea is present above and not fully
Under control. The cloud or bird
Is in its water trough.

Who emerged from the abandoned office.
Something must go, and that thing
Might include what it must leave behind.
Courage, young hero,

Talk about the light in this place
It's fuming. Can light do that?
There is a field in the field leaning forward,

Self-Portrait in a Convex Mirror 2

Pointing off to where they had led them
To a passage, conveniently enough located

On the map. "Like an eagle
That one always sees,
Whether you're there or not
To see it alighting on some rock,"
You can hide yourself like prey
From yourself having been given
The technology. In this way a mirror

Can be a hat or an advantage.
They looked the general in the face,
And it moved. Time was time
In place. Meanwhile, there was a meeting
Held about the fur of a cat in the sun
Somewhere in a room full of children
Or members of congress lost in thought.

There is a room in some American town
Where you can sit, loaf, imagine, etcetera.
There's an ending in thought there,
A feeling all the while: a not uncertain thing
That lingers in the generative possibilities
of toys being put away for once, finally.

15

We repurposed the world again
And left out what didn't grow there.
I feel like being naked to myself
Like a nun without her habit, just
Some ordinary person in the flowers.

There's the light again
With its ultimate assurance
That things don't totally blow.
"Like an eagle
Who hangs out and then suddenly eagles."

Self-Portrait in a Convex Mirror 2

Everything seems to mention itself
The way people are trees of people
Connected through days as if by a force
Of some huge version of spring let out
That held us there.
The gala did what it set out to.
Of all the others, we keep
The air of uncertainty in the air
Of such a place as this the longest.
Monday brings its lunch to the track-meet, and Tuesday
Grows a little inside itself, perhaps in dedication
To a reference we stood without, hoping
To stop all these expectations at last
Where once there'd been a reunion
Scattered from some poorly made picnic area
By some cruel person who changed your name
—But for which purposes,
And at what time of day?
We had gotten ahead of them
Who were called ourselves
Which in theory allowed us to establish
A rude splendor at our muted arrival
Later in the full season.

Who announced us at last?
I had a feeling, but you had multiple
Directed at a likable enough sort
Of being just around the corner.
To our surprise: there were more
Than enough of whichever anyway.
At the showdown, it's better that water
Emits from a human place
Instead of up from an abstract source,
Better that you vomit out the window
Than wait and forget to evacuate.
Measurer, there is a marble dust
That exceeds its power to evoke
What thoughts removed us of our columns.
Everything returns to a humbler time,
Easier-to-grasp because it's now.
You walked down some runway, haply.
We ate to approach the satisfaction
Of a horse eating grass in a field
In the horse capitol of the world.
If one picks luck up if only to carry it
Over there to be set down,

Then there was an honor
To it marked as such.
After all, the dogs must be taken out

Self-Portrait in a Convex Mirror 2

Of their little houses and walked
However strange the season and to whatever purpose
For those who'd ordered it to occur,
Them being, after all, the imponderables.
Finally, you've discovered the possibility
In its entire state, presented to you
Reasonably enough, as if they had known you
To be of what nobility wanted you to be of:
One of those who could always have
Part of what was a really nice time
Despite the occasional accidents. The caravan was lost
In a larger caravan. They put all the small versions
Of everyone down directly. They continued
Behind open doors, doing business
With nobody or with some bored clerk.
All at once it was good to see everything
In its place, at least in a fleeting way,
Us combining into the inventory
Of a system made of various statuses
Beneath the larger idea of our thoughts arriving
On time to act assistants
To the surgery of them
Who weren't risking the chance
Of understanding these made objects
In a formed way. One womb is as good
As a mother. Things can be born

Meaningfully enough to justify a life
Of indecision but just that. Or it was
In our wake we became a topic
Of the conversation we'd begun
All along. It was only
To reach the mirror-world
As a common bird reaches its function

Of a primary nature first and then flight
That we did it. One sustains one.
Things have gotten a little tawny. There are choices
To what we currently live in;
One chooses his or her pony
At the age which is most appropriate
To his or her situation. In agreement,
The committee stands to leave but is arrested
Suddenly by the idea of chance's ubiquity
At this particular moment, unaddressed
Or about to be or finished having been
That and now returning
To guard its precedents. Everything is
Forthcoming if not necessarily at-hand
Like a storm lantern in the coats
Or the word you looked up the other day
Necessarily. I had forgotten that and other things,
Having taken part in a small way in bringing in

Self-Portrait in a Convex Mirror 2

An era of new trails, of paths which don't stop
When you want them to. Then again
We swore off all our strong emotions
Sometime during the deluge. The new animals
Elude their progress in a half-dark.
My whole plan was to muster
Up some history and then unwind,
In a general way, so as to finally relax
And apply the thing I inevitably learned in my respite
To an attempt at humanizing the situation,
So there can be more of us with our brief trips out
To gather the wreckage in advance of going in
And up, resurfacing like a face in the pool.
Certain buildings house marine life
That can speak. Now I must fret about concepts
Even when the sky gazes back at me like a swimmer
Who can look, though it hurts a little, eyes open
At the outstart, moving blankly through the pond.
That adds one more thing to my docket
Of growing duties to accomplish through the gratuitous labor
Of my inner mass elected to present to you
An individual treatment that rejects just such
Simulations, in such parks, before such an audience.
Someone mentioned the thing itself.
That became inadequate. We read our instructions
Together and decided to do all that exactly

As it'd been pre-planned by the original chamber
Of constituents who wrote down what we should've done
In order to leave us questioning the merits
Of originality and begin to establish
The new things in their opposite formations.
One stationmaster said as much
As soon as we landed, emergent on our final prow,
Led by an urge we called fortune
And insisted on doing so,
Though the indefinite is always of a wisdom
If one that outweighs its bearing
Only to topple into the piazza
During the winter festival.
There is no use trying to escape,

Which is the same thing as having reached
An end to our reasons and an engagement
With the world of viewers we'd been inducted into,
For sure. Everything has the license
To approach itself with a handmirror
And look. It is moving, though we didn't want it to
Until someone suggested an acquaintance
With which to settle down in the upstart bar
Or restaurant named after you. You were
Left idling across the way, mentioned in every diary,
Reapportioned to meet the requirement of the ceremony

Self-Portrait in a Convex Mirror 2

Of an adorable system which had been
Etched on the bathroom walls with a knife.
The natural elements persist, even though
There is no place to go to, and there hasn't been
One of those since the early ages
Of a minor relevance which has long been set
Into a history enhanced by its fulfillment.
Us being in the valley, potentially, all along
Given to the ephemerality of one estranged
In the movie-houses, we privately counted one thing
In April after the next. The future rushes out
From its midnight stables, like a color we'd invented
To represent our collective feeling that falls under
The same category as gum and other textural
Experiences in this interrupted geography.
If I were to read Surrey on a patio
After all this time having haven't
Been a man of letters or of men
The process could easily corrupt itself
The way the strange dolls elaborate this impenetrability
Of surface with their glances. All came to it
Rising out of some not insignificant gesture
That we'd mentioned out of habit,
And out of that same thing,
We avoided cataloguing the archive.
Don't think about it in the community.

Some version of the word "cock" alighted
Like a bird, indefinitely if also certain
Of the small ways we go to each other
Naturally as a branch goes to its version of 'up,'
But what would it really do there
If the plans we set out to accomplish became their accomplishment
As fluently as language in an unnamed garden
Burdened with moisture despite its umbrella?
Your portrait cannot stay the subject
Of our advances upon the description of these happenings
Wrested from their ideas involving the true option
That it could very well be contained here.
Not far off in the distance
You approach the chance Cape with
The chance question. The real problem became
Who would be our guests to be prepared
For their imminent departure. The solution did not require us.
It gathered the right things into exclusion
Having already made formal arrangements.
Ask the forest creature about its preference
And the treatment of the crowds of fauna let out
At your high school graduation ceremony if only to prove
Some theory of style or some organic grouping of thought,
Them being raised for said purpose

Self-Portrait in a Convex Mirror 2

Which is what went unsaid after all
Like the teachings we collected insubordinately
From the idea of the cow's whiteness breeding
Patience in its field. A gas became made perhaps
For a perfume or perhaps for nothing.
One experiment suggested you take on Van Doren in the warehouse,
Full of garnet and rose-colored signs for various enclosures
And for the transportation of us from our angst-laden selves
Into a wider form of captivity
Like what they put this audience—who'd traveled
Such a short time to arrive upon it—into.
We needed some more razz-ma-tazz,
Someone insisted at the palladium
Without offering much in the way of a solution
Despite the blatant need for one.
Things got misty outside, but luckily we'd advanced far enough
From the station to forego the sight of all these petunias.
The windows got fatter. I made a pronouncement,
But that wasn't enough to make up for the reception
Which carried on into the wee hours, a symbol of progress,
The morning light of our future grandniece's cabin
Seeping in like a draft so that we may be looked on
With the gaze of one partially asleep. The section leader
Buried one foot in the sand, lifting her golden flag for a while,
And then for a long while. The coastal feeling overwhelmed its visitor
Who hadn't fully understood what it meant to be an arrivant
Or that crouched victor of history the sea suddenly in its place.

Poem in Three Parts 2

1. Love

"Once I went gay-for-pay,
Or I guess currency is flexible—
It was more of an act of bartering:
A service for a gift economy.
A blowjob can be cinematic
Depending on who possesses the camera,
And how they evolve the audience's gaze
To engage whichever preference
As if progress could be what we did by loosening
The coin from where it'd been lodged
Into its cache. These clouds look like
There are more clouds than there are."

The grasses do not get to keep
Their new names prisoner
In this place that's been undrained since spring
Set up its marsh. I wasn't in the mood for camping.
We entered into the customs of a society
That stirred in the blue margin.
One job is probably as good as another,
Despite one being the subtle assignment
Of a beggar: to grow these prairies
From these places led out to by these inlets.
Our subconscious had something to do
With the underbrush, the old cars, and the savages

Who make a home made of them
That is a tower where we regret
How things like time get fatter.
There is at least one reason
The knowable stays that way,
So we made a little list.

2. Courage

Where I was in plaid,
They put me to the discovery of an apartment
In which one could linger unharassed
By the occurrences that went before us—
There where they collect, not unpleasantly,
Like these window plants which have become
Quite the crowd. There's so much
We could do here. So many
Things elaborate on the fact
Of their modesty. Our torque has increased.
Average debris is relatively useful
For the purposes of our demarcation
Which are constant purposes we took on.
At the first chance, I moved into a tree
In order to combine our differences.
Being a talking tree isn't difficult,
But what should I say to myself?

3. I Love the Sea

These predetermined days keep happening
To themselves and to people
We knew from our salad days together
Spent attached to some aimless riverboat.
There is no direct means necessary
But many ways to witness the yellow plains
In combination, one land moving up
Past the massless division.
They have lived there together,
So we will talk about it, relighting
The stove despite being matchless
In the days, or on them, feeling
Particularly retrospective having gathered
Up our sasses to parcel them out
To the met hour and the unmet
Ones in the side yard.

There is a plant blanketing
The garden wall. There could be fruit
There. In one dream, we culled our resources,
Despite the colonel, the dark forest,
And the roads piled up into a city
Of citizens looking over there at the same time
The last piece moved into
The blindness of the idea of noon.

That they set out was not a surprise,
But what they returned to continued to be
Despite everything remaining only imitations
Of a hat or some other human accessory
Put to use. A few fortune-tellers will tell you

Just the basics. That's what we wanted anyway,
Having been threatened with the possibility of a light
That could not be turned off, that would signal
The giant wheel's beginning. If early spring
Insists, one must start its festivals.

Certainly, there's a little darkness
To every square bargain. The distant corners
Get cut off, which you should've expected,
Given the steadily increasing nature of our domain
And the borderlessness of modern cartography.

Everything has reached the long-awaited point
Of saturation and shines there like a set
Of new teeth, left out, washed and ready,
A golden being, bristling and alive, removed
From its oceanic stupor. The way they deliver

One thing after the next, you couldn't stop
For the alarms, let alone the precautions.

Before now is a time all to itself
And to those who made it before now,
Though we were among them. Or so they say.

Perhaps the immediacy of a decision can't do that,
That being any number of things—which is to suggest
We began our little wanderings
Under an unclouded sky, with the morning
Doing its thing with said absent clouds.

Perhaps everything is wanted. Perhaps they put it there
In the orchard to disguise what it really is
Or what it would be were it two people
Giving off the quality of a new planet
That distinguishes itself in part by its culture

But mostly just by being found.
Ideally, our chimeras avoided any drama
That might interrupt this discovery
Of us concluding, in front of a mirror,
One thing: at least we're here.

Suppose a forest-person existed
Who reminded us of why we lived
In a city, protected against the reports of variety
In the green levels. We shall soon be inhabited,
Beside ourselves. We shall wrestle a little.

Self-Portrait in a Convex Mirror 2

The hooves beat under the control of their giraffes
Or something more mysterious, above all this
And unarmed. The castle couldn't stand
To border more than one magical forest
Which turns into whatever you point to.

We're here, and so is the dog—
Which is nice. Dying couldn't be half-bad
If this were its introduction, though I've been fooled
Before; though when I was, I enjoyed it a little
Or someone told me to.

If a voice calls out, and those rooks do
Along with it, we could call that
A proclamation of all our senses,
Blessed by sight under such a vault
As this one—which remains slightly ajar.

After all, there's no reason the villagers
Can't respond. An event is made up of
Bees and other animals—ones set loose
Beside the lake, which keeps lengthening,
Over the years, as if to move a boat.

Farm 2

The contract began somewhat sporadically
Involving the land animals' removal
From plain-life to life at the agency
That bridges one thing from another.
Our status felt unnatural.
We drew a force from the property
Of course, but that didn't mean anything
When it came to be about an emotional attachment
To the physical partition that exists
Uninjured by sight and our escape plans.

So we left the city for once
In a steadfast manner with the new girl
Who established that white fences exist
And that the comings and goings would
Do just that. Poppies and irises
Negate them. The purple of the ages
Calls for you, wretchedly. Few enough
Get out, but this was their season
With you amongst them. There was one
Who hadn't been excused to be there.

Now that they've found
Another use for ferns
        that they'd forgotten about
They'll grow foreign in the public world
That gently houses our militia.
One product of memory associated itself
With the blue documents
The tinmaker'd drawn up. Frontiers
Can't adjust to their errors. The study room
Fills up with boys,

And there was some information available,
But mostly we came to
Simultaneously in a position
Of grace, with one leg asleep.

I signed up for
A time at the center.
I would've liked to prepare myself

Prior to this evening's lattice-work
Was constructed across the road
To distinguish the creatures through it
From the forestry they ravaged
In becoming that indecorous sort
Of workmen of departing carriages

of a burnt dusk.
They whistled all at once, though the temple was closed
And thus the proposal along with it
Which had been for the time being.
But nothing doesn't fumble
Or make a likeness.

There are little versions of water
That attack you
Irreversibly in a motion
Given to them, almost articulately,
And then go back to water.

What was dark was the fluidity of these situations
And of the almanac they used to predict them.
Surely we'd have composed ourselves
In another time just as wildly
Extravagant if also suddenly
As a mouse's lisp in the corn. Fractions
Are baby numerals. The fecundity
Of whole systems rises. Ol'
MacDonald, carry off your answers
Into the fermenting gardens as if
Catapulted by a straw from its shake.

Hop o' My Thumb 2

At the grand estate, the great dairy
Has sent its representative dancers in
To do what they do. But to whom?
Our calendars have been devised
To present the luxury of these boys,
Whether or not their names are made public
And Undine is left there like a used coat.
Everyone needs to scuttle
Once in a while and right now particularly.
Someone's flopped over the balcony.
The notes go on being unread and steeped
In liqueur, through the leveling storm,
Thrown up from the bullpen
The orchestra has made its base.
Stay unspoken, like a cream
Dropped into the foliage
Amidst all this hubbub about something
You dreamt of having to do with dice.

It all comes out automatically
Like a plush doll in a firestorm.
What you described wasn't your enchantment,
But the way you did it was.
First and foremost, the clamor drew
Its arrow from the apple on top of all this
And into the noon moment.

Self-Portrait in a Convex Mirror 2

We unwedged ourselves from a crevice
Which we had lived in, disdaining
The horizontal. Hurry up, feathered diva,
And strike. The world is unbounded,
Or such was the world they put away
To be retrieved at a later event, past chaos
And this museum we haunted in.

All our implied children will be ruined shortly
In such a controversial environment
Designed to create the people's distractions
Gracefully. You set out a plate of milk
To draw something less common than
The fairy swarm. It was impossible
To locate what was calling, "Ariadne. Ariadne,"
In the outdoor hall of mirrors
Where you led your sisters back
To the place they'd dreamed of being twins
At night, arranged into a working system
Which lifted its apex above the spot
You'd imagined so carefully, laid into
The doorway like one of time's nurses
Striking the bell twice to signal
Where things had been presupposed
To arrive, to live on sherbet, and then just to live on.

Everyone saw herself, the way one sees anything:
Nested into a gestural perception—
But then the world doesn't resemble a curtain
Or an individual lair you forgot you'd made
Where there was already a hole.
To follow every stage direction at once
You must first form a sphere together
Of a human scale hitherto unknown
And since made so by a physicality
With little function but to trace
Its interests into the string matrix
Of some bird whose name we forgot
But whose face we just couldn't.

I don't get people from Boston
Who stay there but find the ones
Who leave it to be fair examples
Of the times and their precedents, if made
Slightly baby-esque by this old notion
Of getting younger slowly.

Elevators get a bad rep
Like the half-nudes who descend in them,
Centauri, topless and natural as the lighting
When it gets dark around itself.
Some policemen have small cars

To patrol around in. Skeeter, I whispered
To you in the steeple. Regarding the Mugwumps,
You suggested a new episode that could be
The final hour of us at last that had been
Projected to occur, shortly, like a presence.
Fewer things happened that made a boat.

Taking a path of kindness to know
What that is like, they drew you
As if in sleep, removed from description,
"To be traveling always, affixed between
A routine and the unscheduled finale
The gaffers whispered of behind us."
After all, thunder is a sufficient means
Of proving the existence of electricity
In it and all this talk.

Foreboding 2

We entered Luna Park necessarily
Passable for deer who enter
Dressed in single-piece outfits—
All of us like a daylit brigade
Of petals in the saloon.
The management was comprised of grown men
In braces, beating the hell out of the situation
And its bike messenger. The jungle emptied
Its pockets as if to become partially
What was the yet-to-be-determined.
One equation resulted in a soft moment
Uninjured by division and bought
Like a small, difficult-to-eat fruit.
A wave occurred simultaneously.
I said, "There will be no more
Reportage of us, Excalibur.
When things get settled, I'll go on.
But until that wandering attendant
Returns to this rarer order
That exists between my nocturnal life
And anybody else's, nothing will."

Self-Portrait in a Convex Mirror 2

It is the first good noir of the year:
It's you, at the party, with the plants.

The hydrangeas don't protest
As fluently as Satie in the gardens
Only just barely guarding us
From our suburban games.

The Hooples are sleeping by the pool.

I'm thoroughly exhausted by the Major
And his emittance of lilacs:
There will be no postures
Worth shifting the natural mirror to meet
Until you strike them.

Meanwhile in Tokyo,
One gumshoe after the next
Had the idea to start up as a detective
And become something else, an investigation
Of the amphitheater or of something in it
There that was Greek to us.
They put you down into the scenery
At the time of the assignation of parts
Until you could be picked up. Bees do this,
Continually making some honey or some jubilee

Pinched into the landscape's waist
That divides the upper world
From its moving parts.
She said she wanted "a wanted thing."
He wanted everything lovely.

"I have become accustomed to your style. It seems that by taking a process
of inquiry into a practice, of literature as such, you've adjusted what
meaning can do. There is the place of the poems that you return to by read-
ing them as gestures—that cannot be gathered, though our thoughts
linger with them."

"It would be unforward of me to avoid wanting more in the way of an
explanation of how the magnet sits, establishes a repulsion in the verse,
all the while static in these shifts."

The plush world sinks
To its subterranean door.
One beats one's tin drum to request
Entrance to Pachelbel's house.
How about a newly hermetic arrangement
That withdraws its suffering for once?

Come on down then
Before the past lets out.

Self-Portrait in a Convex Mirror 2

Because it lifts the fragments to an order
That is almost perceptible in these mistakes
Of the architect made dangerous
To the witnesses of this construction
Of the temple out back,
One piece is added to another.
What it's like gets difficult
As our lives persist in arriving
At every place equally as the floods.
Something is ready to coagulate:
"Father! Come back," one cries.
Father: "'Come back,' cried something."
I knew you were there
All along in the blue places of the Aegean.
Seeming to have returned is another way
Of being here for a while, like a master
Of the outdoors going inside.

Easing something
Into the late afternoon's
Store of space in relation
To this vision's dwelling
Where the creatures go
In as if to signal,
Some power was
Just before it is.

They thought themselves too much
Acquainted with their seasonal
Removal from the wet industry,
Or rather placed beside it,
Two picnickers blessed by them
And losing the thought carefully
Like a scientist in the river sent
To be their blind guest
As the center keeps forming
Only to the situation
That knows it and to no other
Abstraction suggesting, "Things have gotten
Too soon." All things should be
Sent back—except the hawks—
Without us to the city.

Mixed Feelings 2

A thing exists to itself
In any state, lifting up to you its thingness
Like the symmetrical body of a fighter pilot
Leaning on the body of his government jet,
The times spent past our due recognition
Of these Lts., of these Captains of them,
Fierce ones put to the earth by a force of pride
At being grounded in the senses made up
By me in my overalls, asking the one on the left
To go to a small vintage 1947 café
And begin a career solving crimes like P.I.s in PEI,
Except that by belittling me, we could both escape
The expectations of our routine flirtation
At the garden center, picking up one vegetal fabric
After the next, examining our hobbies
In the light of these normal prospects
Of becoming those of a higher class, to go on
Draped in the imaginary scenery of California.
Aw nerts, was that Donald Duck? It wasn't.
Then why is it that they boarded us into
Our mutual crate but to be a single thing
Shipped out by whoever it is who reads mail
Not without thinking but at the same time
Not really being ready to shift to the extremes
Of the possibility of us meeting our relevant data
With its relevant researchers in the field.

Self-Portrait in a Convex Mirror 2

They do look, at least, like they could look at you,
As you babble on about the sky's demands
Of total disclosure in its ballpark
Creating, at least for these moments, an inner life.
Things were cute in a devastating way.
I was funny-ish about all of this before,
I who had once abandoned all feelings
In order to interrupt the ships of us set out
After living around here for quite some time
On images alone. If the muse orders the day's
Cavalry into a starred formation that can be seen
From this view, where everything makes its own
Forest of change, all my horses better hurry.

Now we knew each other formerly
As the police knows the shifting states
In you who belong to this living world,
But shut up about it already.
How should a mandate go?
I'm going to throw my selves a party,
One by one.
You go to the interstices
To see the newly discovered plant
In the open. Apparently,
It's bad luck to compare hands.

There are parts of America
We leant to ourselves like these
Funerals with the ceremony withheld
That nonetheless form a beige shell
You'd crack out of except it was actually
A wooden egg we emerged from to speak
Softly, the way trees can be soft,
Though these tendencies strike us
As being increasingly common
If rare as a raspberry in water,
Hidden deep in the kitchen,
Us just having left the house.

Self-Portrait in a Convex Mirror 2

I know I put together these,
Whatever they are, too often to notice
An abridgment beneath the privacies
Of an older version of what will be.
When do things boom like a small bell,
Crushed underfoot, into instances of kindness
That comprise them? When does destiny
Tower in its remote orchard
If not always, to be reached by you
Who's pinpointed the root?

You have to be tender enough
To unhinder this conceit, gone rampant,
Of volatility being an indoor thing
And the rest being where the rest lands.
It is all of the trials that tell us
To be known. One fate was behind the curtain
You pushed aside to see the letter
Addressed to you, if illegibly so.
Day after day, time obscures you,
This being a natural effect the message
Has tried to evoke, the papers ripped
From their envelope, now and in the future,
In the cool yards, fenced in by a previous tenant
Of this home that is yours
Besides being small and in the country,
Our country, and from the streets.

I will begin to tell you
About the scalawags at the harbor
As if this interruption were welcome
And the boats a blue sort of red
But also red—not to alarm you.
They're still there anyhow.

What you didn't teach me
About sex as we know it
I learned like a blind person taught to play
The church organ, which is, by the way,
A topic of conversation I much enjoy
Despite its growing popularity in the cities.
You look like a young Bret Harte,
But I'm too cotton-eyed to know better
Here with my duchesses. Some people
Don't look like they should. I should
Know better or else give thanks,
But I'm not sure what to.

There are folks in my neighbourhood
Who share a connexion
That is somewhat unflattering, but to whom?
Really, I'd rather be Virginia Woolf
Than myself, if I could retain
This sentience I've learned to take some pride in

Like a true nature. What we have
Does not escape us by definition,
But that, as we know, is a slippery notion.
The honor system is a little like vision.
I'm really seeing things, repetitiously
In the landscape, behind the school,
That look like me. I'm free
Much of the time to appreciate
My own interests, but they don't get to.
You put a wall up around the perimeter
And shirk what's coming in
Or what tries to this fine afternoon.
You imagine a violist gone unchecked,
Forming her musical nuisances,
And we ready ourselves to receive
The canceled program, penultimately.

So anyway, the message goes
Unexplained, except that we said it
To you, this brave audience
I plan to talk to again
And kind of am doing so already.

Leading in from the foliage is
Another activity of the dark philosophies
I subscribe to—oh stop! The problem is
That of obscurity in the frog moment,
In its green way, in the spell of said juncture.

The distance doesn't count for much
To "the machines" that line their shore
Of what turns out to not be an actual lake
But something partially made into one.
To do art—and here some take liberties
In defining their contemporary practice
As such—is to forget the remainder,
Indigent of color, like rabid impressionists
Floating off somewhere that is nature,
With the notion of finding a stone tree.

I don't know what I tripped on
On my trip to Autumn Lake,
But I'll gather several natural antidotes
Just in case—preparing for the dead end
We expected like a weather report.
If I sound foreign, it's a mistake
Of the distillation of sound in music
That can be studied, like the way that
There are intersections.

Self-Portrait in a Convex Mirror 2

What isn't me is starting
To exist again. I haven't
Redrawn the boundaries at all,
And now the project is late,

But that's how we should've wanted it.
The piano inhabits its space about itself
Like skirts hovering above you
As she says, "John, don't look."

A little Poulenc… and then
The sound breaks from its hinge,
Because it has to. I do things that way,
For the old reason, indefinitely.

The barrier is blocking the attic door,
But all that was stored there never meant much
To us in our rambling ways
On some balcony we stood on at the time.

You make the necessary salutations: "Hello.
What are you?" There were two of me,
I thought I knew, foreshortened,
And a quietness that took to being words.

Ode to Bill 2

Time takes up a lot of itself,
And then we are left with what we do
To it and to the uses we put it to
Quite naturally in a field. Clocks
Gather inland. They care only enough to be asked.

Or, for example, I wanted to write
Last month and did, but one increase
Met its other. It involved ideas
And saying what I meant to do
With all these thoughts like a nonentity
Used for processing great tasks. What do I mean?
Don't go there. It's not today enough.

There is something I feel
Has happened to what I'd first put on
In jest to entertain an imaginary passenger
As we drive out into the agricultural district.
One way to look at yourself
Is to always do that, with pleasure,
Since that's what the Sun does.

At least the century exists.
My distractions are getting violent
In a purple way. The land goes on receiving
Other visions, having forgotten its ticket to a chaos

Self-Portrait in a Convex Mirror 2

That refuses to linger. Everybody's dead
Before too long. I thought I told you that
In the slack belly of our hours,
When we were sunny or the world was.
Things wander off slowly again. Bill asks,
"What was the question?"
And tomorrow pivots.

Lithuanian Dance Band 2

Larry the Great would be a good name to reintroduce
Into this world the idea of drama and a general weight
That seeps into fruit gradually causing the pit to drop
Sowing this chaos that we've grown accustomed to overriding
As when a wounded human or animal drives back to safety
Only to draw its predators out on the cave wall

I am writing to you standing here where you are
Breathing as impossibly as it is to make money
I don't know what the beginning of wwi was like
But let's take some time like right then right now
And reinsert it into all kinds of new delicacies
Of thought come forth to support these acts
Of concentration and toast us through their teeth

Something takes on the form of know-how if a damaged one
That has broadened itself to match today with uncertainty
Like a whole era drifting in a cordial modus operandi
All the while, keeping it up from some impetus
To shoot death down with a gun and watch it
As we said we would at the projected moment
Of our arrival into some good that makes just that happen

The truth arrives a little uncultured
And true, which is refreshing—to have someone deliver us
For once from our difficult task in the unlit ballroom

Self-Portrait in a Convex Mirror 2

Where they strike up the orchestra on a moving platform
Built to make it an eligible participant in this parade of thoughts
And march down Washington Ave., all the while seated
Atop a triumphant day set forth from the changing light
Into that that stays brilliant amongst the army of dancers
If there were sex in friendship, this would be its place
Right here on the floor strewn with bells
So that you know where you are at each moment
Without having to look too closely, thus being able
To surrender to yourself in this changing climate

One day you might expect to be looking back
And realize how the lines pointed off to what you put there
At the end of them that you could somehow divine
As separate from the world with its preposterousness
Spinning in an old sound at the reaches of the wind
The directions buried under this thick gloss
By an expert who'd set the final touch long ago

Death may not be necessary to a full life
Yet certainly it wants you there part-time
You work yourself up into a tizzy alone
And being with people is a constant duty
Therein comprised of whole landscapes of beauty
That surprise you like most things always do
Like a crow riding on the back of an eagle

Sand Pail 2

Progress
leads down the red road jutting
out from its environmentally viable
windmills as we approach.
A marker
directs traffic from the center
of these crocuses in the piazza at night
by a sort of curving. The situation exits.
Why don't we do the same?
A development can involve digging, "they" say;
uninterrupted filters do;
moments of capital
depict you on a beach.

And then? The certainty of colors
And their rescue in language?
And the marching band at the track meet
Hurried to music? A blur on the concrete
Shifted like a biker into second gear,
Assigning all the other cyclists new names.
Yes, most likely. We were just waking up
In a dream, having partially invented the world.
Everything gets carried off in the end
But not to anywhere in particular; the exact
Spot doesn't matter on the surface of a flood.
When it wasn't a holiday, we waited around
In line for the next event when everybody
Gets decorated like every landscape does
Naturally. We designed our own garments
To adjust to these new domains. Sweden
Can't not be about itself, even occasionally.
One page turns out to be an old road map.
I can't speak to the business of minding
Myself until the precise moment shows itself
Unencumbered by vegetation, in my life.
The English lessons go on, undisturbed,
But something gets in—yes, the character
In a novel, meaning one thing the way a fragment gathers
With its others to do just that. The fact that
We draw flowers is to say that anxiety exists

As a metaphor before it does this morning.
I've worked on the influences, precariously,
Shifting from one foot, zeroing in on the edge
Where we add up the binary systems and expect
To find this or that. I need a job while I'm alive
Teaching starving people how to eat again
In the field we turn into a cafeteria
And live in it like a sleepy chef.
I can do what I want if that's just sitting
Hhere on the bench, lifting—at best—
Two arms. Under the lunch table,
Light collects somehow. Add it all
Once and that will be where we start
To witness the neighbors stretching their red tape
To meet the inaugural days and push them back.
Time-wise, I'm more interested in being close to the finale
Such that they tell you, "Here it comes."
I pulled an apocalyptic prophecy from my pocket
In this passage that is the whole world.
A perfume is drenched in itself, inherently.
At the reception, we met our dance partner
And went from there. Dying should happen
With a handshake on the bench at sunset,
Our human ferality preserved like a silk cross
Pressed between the pages of a book. The opacity
Of plant life ruins itself in just a little heat.

Self-Portrait in a Convex Mirror 2

For memory's sake, we've gotten close enough
To say that, anyhow, in the late evenings.

Give us our snapdragons with the children's
And ward off all else like a doctor who is loved
Bending backwards to retrieve the dial
That's come off. You can monitor
Almost anything, and so we come to our heroine
Expecting to do that, until she turns invisible,
If accidentally so, like the time she did it in
That also did that. I miss that time. Our totality
Breaks out into a feeling and shudders in
The lobby of its subtropical casino.
I need a doctor who can renew
My prescription to drive in the country.
(Waterford spontaneously combusted.)
The meadows became implicated in the mood
Of trial and other smaller bits of emotion
That point to the fact that you have stayed on
Supplying a theory of friendship that favors
Rest in each other's arms during the giant
Form of twilight that's begun to peel off. You should
Spend the afternoon retracing a branch pattern
That stopped the light from hitting the floor
To create a stopped version of the reflection
Of solidity as it moves before we do. One solution

Would be to ban camaraderie and woven things
And listen to the old LP with your other favorites
Becoming fantastic as the savages
Whose money is dead. There is a stimmüng.
A chair lengthens in its days to be just that.

The singularity calls out from its space
To meet you, but you're too sleepy
And all too familiar with the notion
Of everything clustered into a silver dew,
Unable of itself.

This wasn't supposed to be the distillation
Of history. Or they will all share
A memory wherein the lag occurs in
Its depictedness. Various measures collapse
Like a girl in a raincoat at the gate.

Every time you describe an 'orange'
Things get more orange and misty.
I'm listening, sure, but who wouldn't?
The pines put this green-black together
In response to the light, mastering
Nature. Doing nothing else is nice.

The snow gets in, unable to do much
But melt at the door. You unbuttoned love
From its cloth shelter—or so you told me,
As if the feeling itself could gain enough
Awareness and say: What you thought I was,
I was. Go on and tell you about yourself,
Reviewing the final report with interest
As they place it in the whole archive.

Märchenbilder 2

Es ist ein stein...no, it's too weightless
To be that. It'd break if it ever landed, and besides
Your geology sucks. To put it differently:
"Rain elaborates on the color of the earth

Which is a sort of blue-gray, like how a newspaper
You made into a boat, like its news, absorbed
By the fountain, looks tinted." Tell me how
Lace lengthens like a Queen named Anne,

Stretched out as a canvas lounge chair,
Hand-made from a music made textile.
A whole sonata got away without knowing
Anything, because everybody wanted it to.

A cluster of black notes on the blank page
Reveals its future pattern, like a sound catching
Up to what was just wind in the woodwinds.
Who is this speaking anyway all of a sudden?

The flower expresses its flower-ness
At dawn as if to gather in fields
Is another way of saying, "Yes, please,
Go on." Someone says: "There are those

Self-Portrait in a Convex Mirror 2

Who are actual roses." Night's compact
Is fragile, but we don't have a rock
Or even a drink to throw into its face.
We've gone into our cave like a tree would,

Half of its branches necessarily left out,
Or like a bullfrog ducked from land to reach
Its dinner of wet rings. The flux remains
To welcome you at this entrance.

I'm thinking of life just a little bit
More than I would were I dead.
For Pete's sake, I died laughing
and was reincarnated that way too.

City Afternoon 2

The air defines what it will air
Out by doing that. By the water,
This tapestry unravels a bit, being
Of unicorns at war with the future dead.

Sometimes I feel this road has little feet beneath it
That go on despite my conveyance of them
Like an America that's walked off-stage
And out into the whole world
Just to show you it could.

The depiction involves garlands
And that the future can change
Waiting for a new currency
To progress like an old skiff
Diagonally in the reflecting pool.

This is how the day would be: forgotten
Except that it rained slightly, like some cologne
You'd meant to buy, suggestive
Of the moment you were meant
To wear it in. The birds are terrible
But not mean, especially
Not to this happiness you put them to.
But probably heaven is sick with fruit and jewels
If not vegetables like hell which is resilient
And does not stray from the outline
Of a collapsed contour drawing, brushed
With oil and burning slightly
Just on the edge of solitude
Having seen it mostly from above
The blanket of fog on the bed
Of fog. Dismissed from the high table,
You rotate down the stairwell as if to decide
Circuitously, this way was worth its pursuit.
Come on down and join the feasting
Grounds scattered with watermelons
In what could've been as still as ice
In the final lemonade you sipped at
Coolly, clean as a wick that's about
To be lit, time speeding toward us,
The hypothetical value of abduction
Being a means to tug this boat from its clay

Mire that you reported to with your lantern
At the ready. Who were those people?
The twenty-nine of them dimming
The manor for some party
In a manner parallel to the rate
At which you think of steepness
Mounting the side of this roundabout palace
At an angle they determined to be purely aesthetic.
Serenity is the dumb luck
You rushed to meet the "How are you?"s with
And turn the conversation to the future years
That rise into probability
Before anyone can stop them and snuff this burning
Forest which will phoenix—again.
We're probably a herd of deaf bears
Circling home like a voluptuous moon
Pulled to what waters shall know it
Though you dare not to.
I am not the honored guest
They called you to greet. Quite possibly,
You are, and that would make me
And light something else that mothers
And protects this errant climate.

Self-Portrait in a Convex Mirror 2

And some had cognizance
Of being in the situation until there was no more
Coming out of it to take on
What was outside of this, the polite
Intelligence going out of its way
To be what was to be described
And human if only momentarily.

Our motivations should be honorable
And small, like the dew that nags at the edges
Promoting a gesture of water—the tragedy
Being that death shouldn't exist until you look
Old-fashioned, delivering your parcel
At dawn, wrapped in a black embroidery.
The stitches involve your dotage.

A climate of change can be lived in
Despite the proprietary nature of these shifts
Towards a suburb made entirely of weather
Or something more annual than that
Which the kids are into, in cycles,
One building managing to hide its territory
Just by being there, and one not.

But I meant to arrive at a law
By generalizing: this is the Sun

And nothing has such a constant practice.
Helplessly, the noises await their orchestra,
And the dancers get skittish on ice.
The company continues, its mission being
To be both temporary and complete. No one

Can access the palladium anymore or its station
Which housed nothing but a history of trains
And even that just briefly. Gray flags
Still haunt this place, standing for one thing
After the next. Everything was useful.
Sweetness knocked one time just to say
There's a woodruff in the strawberries.

Remember what gathered or don't,
It still did, emblazoned on a shield
Like the majesty of a dead friend,
Like a word that requires no tending
To by your lips, just time's maw
Or tongue sliding out to check
If what's incubating there is edible.

Don't sense or know anything
Today, and the directions might show themselves,
Unwieldy things they are that want an army
Of them to conquer this pale world

Self-Portrait in a Convex Mirror 2

And place their completed work on a dais.
I wanted the environment to dream again,
So I built its carrier.

To manage the blank spaces they made
Something mild and arranged,
Starting with the ground and going
Up. Yes, we were waiting.
No, this is our stop.

After all that it takes
A while before starting
To know that it already did.

I beg of you.
Listen to me, I beg of you.

The first thing shuts
But not down irremediably

Like an accident
That accidentally happened
                          thus.

But the novel is one
In which we shouldn't bet
On a single probability to answer
The question of what

Self-Portrait in a Convex Mirror 2

Will get done.
Luckily, you could know
That life would play its part
And come up to you.

You followed the elf to a crossroads
Where she turned into an eagle or sign
And left you like two arrows shot
In either direction. One led
Back to the well-furnished studio
Where they design aquatic wallpaper
For use in beachside hotels (the sink
Is a seashell; the floor's made of seashells.)
Things have been transient, which allows you
Free range in the second world
Of green flowers and secretaries
(With their guest appearances.)
Everything was a facade there, even the water
Of life which has been stolen
(But you'll find out. It wasn't
Madonna whose last name
You forgot.) Jethro needs your assistance,
And so does the old man
In his inherited kingdom.
Rescue comes late, on page 500,
As you rise from Centreville into the center.

But they took you
From the abiding waters
Like a killer whale
Into a kind of Florida.

Everybody looks for whatever
And will get it
Eventually, such was the strategy

Until everybody
Finally did and being
Thought back to itself
Like it could think
That it would come to this
With its one wheel forever.

The way Parmigianino did it, one hand tied
To something larger, a physical idea brought
As if swerving from the original prospect
As a means of leading off to greatness from behind
The lead panels, no accomplishment can rise
Undivided. The beige window refuses its tilt
Quite possibly. Vasari said he was haunted "to be
As a Raphael come back from his death of which
Little could be depicted but that which came through
This youth, sent to present just such a change in the field
Of sight, pressed as closely to his influence as a moss
In the woods as it gets darker." The wooden ball
Reminded someone of glass—enough at least to attract
The attention of a dream delivered between fits
Of global dimension and flux. The pity of it
Distinguishes those from something able
To advance much further in a single combination
Of events leant to their required properties:
Pleated muslin, fur, the new carpenter's beams
Bending to match the older wood but on realistic terms
That have taken what could be a portrait of size
In gesture if not in surface
Or rather on it and nailed to the silver
World where repetition means prophecy
Transposed at a 180-degree angle in a pre-second.
The glass chose its purpose. It is what is

Sequestered. The density of movement has been fixed
And still understood to be absent as the perspective
Point which draws you, humanely, to this treatment.
The soul exists in its changing limits
That have combined to intercept this picture
Of utter distance divided from its nest
In which the restless passenger steps out
Onto a recurring wave of what's been possible
Only to return to it like the hours spent at his desk
That can now be visited. It must inch
Out to be given even that much space between here
And the general roar suspended at the boundary
Though reasonably unguarded. The work's rules cohere
To form a tenderness so powerful that we are wrenched
From this museum of the moment, our attention staying on
To mingle with remorse for such a place that can be
Described as wordlessly as music, if somewhat bent
All over, the soul kept in its rented apartment
Speculatively (speculum, from the Latin mirror).
But it is life englobed. Darkness resumes
All of its cautious activity at once,
Turning duly away from calculation. Clouds
Can be made to be fragments, can meet their fate
Wildly as the fact that this prison-hold exists
And that surface is always the last structure
To be invented and is the mathematical promise

Self-Portrait in a Convex Mirror 2

Of these counterparts in their dull opera
Of glass and weather, which in French is
Le temps, the word for time. No other
Precision could notate the whole on a plush
Scale set out to be our mutual contract
Drawn up to merge one experience with its last
Thought and thus breed a severity
That is the signal to let consciousness in.
This union has no power, no boss
To determine what will hold or at least
Leave behind the semblances of one made stable
By embracing the affirmation of the painter's sleeping
Quarters laid out before us. There is no subtlety,
Francesco, that fills the alcoves with your giant
Hand, which we look at to be assured
Of our changes. That they have reached the perpetrator
Is all the more reason to suggest stability
Can exist in this vacuum, its ping-pong ball
Still suspended on a jet of water—
Just as there is no apt model
For what's replaced the core purely
To do that and the other work of promoting
The need for a natural embrace
With the estranged apprentice of sight
Which is not the eye but vision's witness
In vision's witness's body.

The gauge is busted or tends to be
When you most need it to measure
How this tiny but important ship won't
Be the same. The particularity reflects
Its bottom, by some subdividing line,
Onto the facing plane which is all too formed
Like a gesture which needs to be reused
If it is to exist as something more
Than a single occurrence of the trigger pulled
To signal the outstart's initial thrust
From its inner chasm into the ridden movement
That buckles against rest
And raises Cain as well as pathos
From some urge to people this range
Of possibility and then self-destruct.
No words to say what could've been
And few to say what is, we go in,
Not dangerously, though the danger lies there
For all its well-rested pioneers who've caught
Hold of a fixed remnant that both
Secures and denies nothing.

The balloon goes suddenly from inflation
Into sound, and all that's reliant
Upon this scatters into the bashful memory
Of your friends who remember there

Casually as a donkey pulls the weight
Of silver and iron or of what
It pulls out from the sawlands
Into this fairer company. How
Many dark or familiar phrases
Have drawn you to turn back from the page
Into a heightening peculiarity
That constructs yesterday's efforts
From a new model of collapse
That stands up, that walks
Backward to match your approach
And lead you or else be beheld
As an influence and fly off breathlessly
From the wet branches. One conceit
Can be felt starting its perverse carousel,
Though it devised no engine to run it
And couldn't distract the gaze
The wanderer sets on his symmetry
To catalog it. Those voices get into
A dusk of sorts and stay put. Books do.
Speed does not. The tale involved you
Sitting still by a neutral magma
And looking in as if you could do anything but that.
The strewn evidence means.
The larger accidents are devoid
Of grace and thus uttered to an audience

That includes a risen chaos. Certainly,
We chased Francesco here
Into this bower and expect
Some transformation, perhaps the classical
One where beauty runs out from civilization
To meet its inanimate habitat
Made of itself now made of
A tree that was a lady once
And more importantly was what was
In between the two of those versions at a point
And perhaps still is. The polestar
Is blind as a painted eye, and yet it sees
The intended portrait better for it
Being so. Ain't that the kicker?
That this reflection surprises us
Obliquely and then again much later
As if it were both the sign
Of a bell and what the bell predated.
Let everything stay foretold
As the day moves on, piling up

The chores of a common system
Of housepeople accomplishing the extraneous
Work of circling this matter
Which grows. "With great art,
To copy all that you saw in the glass,"

Self-Portrait in a Convex Mirror 2

Was what you were to do, you said.
Because these things get parceled
Out to restore the properties
That demand the thoughts that will be
Given to establish a prominence
Of the balled-up course surrounded
By its tensions—to return to
What was its center that must show itself
And be what must hoard
This landscape of attention
Close to the origin of what the artist knew.
There will always be a succession of foci
Letting one ramble on back home
Which is a place between them
And comfortingly so. Tomorrow is easy,
Today uncharted and quite possibly
Of a depth that's being tested, just this once,
But one could grow accustomed to
Waking from the bubble-chamber
Into anything, building, by the handful,
The new countenance. The egg is clustered
Upon a sturdy base, but that does not promise
A single increase of the senses at the display
Of all these fine goods to be traded
At last, but you've no currency
Except that which by keeping what was seen

Sacred in a climate of hesitation
And a transparent smoke, you earn a little. May
Waxes to make the cabbage rose flourish, leaving
Us to guess what season this is,
And of what noble hour? So the room
Contains more than an hourglass
Which varies like the grains it transports
From the flooded attic to where the pile
Suggests it's been put upon
A dreamed cone (except perhaps
It was a triangle, and the plane a contract
Or not perhaps, since this is so—more on this later.)
Enter the slum, follow the sumptuary laws,
And try to shape this habit of leaning
Into recognition. Sydney Freedberg writes
In his *Parmigianino* that "realism loses
Its sobriety but not its form
Which is the ideal beauty of the pursuers
Of an actuality replete as the source of dreams
That cannot take everything and instead
Delivers its account through another."
In the shape of some happy arrangement,
It can sustain its foraging.

As I start to forget
There comes a line straight from the source
Which sounds austere to those
Who can hear it. Riding with enough fury
To unanchor the vehicle, a new ground
Catches beneath our feet but one
That is only there when needed,
Which is always now. A dream includes
Places, though they aren't immediately necessary.
There is a lapse that makes us discoverers
Of what can go missing, which is everything,
Thus all that can be replaced
Is such a number as the one we called out
That grew to match our stereotypical expectations.
There hazards issue from the hundred angles
Of thought present, but you have another
Sort of beauty that comforts you
And allows one "rather angel than man" (Vasari)
To look like everything, or else
Who was who you came across in Naples
Where they held the master's later works
Such as the Uffizi "gentlemen" and the Borghese
"Young pirates," not to mention the *Antaeus* issue, but here
Freedberg suggests there was a surprise to the concept
That should not have been, for the idea
Was based in life. The invention of reason

Took place in the summer of 1959 with Pete
Seeing it in all its urgency in New York—
Not for the first time, for that would involve
Spectacle, but for the second, for it is always
That time that you may see familiarities
In our life, which is an algorithm
Of other occurrences of a similar nature.
It will be hard for you; ending
Anything will be from now on,
At least until late, except that the day
Shuttles off what's been inside
To tell you to do that soon
After its own intentions. Since they are a metaphor
Made to include us, the bare walls question
Why we look at them for solace
But mostly just to question them. Nobody
Comes out the other end changed
Unless we change what we meant by that

And turn the concentric growing out of our days
On its axis. A breeze can make you forget what page
On which you saw it brought back with a lock
This time but one which was turned by Mahler
On his ninth try, as Berg said
Of Imogen in Cymbeline, "There is no
Carrier of death that can't be

Self-Portrait in a Convex Mirror 2

Pinched between the string and the lyre," for
Tactics lead nowhere except waiting,
When the initiate arrives
As hazy as a tooth seen through the glass fog
That you'd hoped would've bitten you.
Whatever vacancy would be my own
I had known elsewhere by consulting
What seemed to distinguish the meaningful escapades
From those that stood outside of time in
That mirrored state, the tributaries broken off
By themselves into a vague permanence
That could shift or was that it did that.
That the room was being empty remains a sign
Of the hosts, because they went to push
Forward, awake and silent about the special reason
Why light communicates more clearly
To those in the midst of a renaissance
Unfolded like a suburb from the otherwise defined city.
This casted twig-shadow is more than a spell
And rather the physical contract that astonishes the church
Before mystics can rush in to explain it.
The sunlight reproduces its lair with an alien's touch
Of accuracy forged from the unfamiliar nature
Of such depiction. It does not show
Or follow the trail you'd set for it
To get to its final escape, which is inevitable.

Instead the exit is immediate, allowing the replaced
Map of the known world entrance.
The collective past shivers where it's led out
But not to portray an emotion,
Though it is good at imitations and nostalgia
Which should be thought of as a love
That mistakes the object for its force.
The long corridor leading to his painting is a part
If not of the whole than of nothing.
But that, like whether the public can shove out
Before the museum closes is almost guaranteed,
Though we prefer that it isn't a little
And that we two passengers can remain
Past the schedule into a reckless appreciation
Of the senses for what gave them.
The substance has no end or record,
The way the sun sounds to itself as it does
To this that can get close enough,
Not a light only but the origin's
Combustion baked into a wielded mass
For the viewer to be able to persist through the day
And then to imitate it, at best, by night,
Listening to the candle as it passes
From one stage and listen when it's out.
The substance has no end or record
Like an aura of creation rather than one given
Off by some locus of daily activity

Self-Portrait in a Convex Mirror 2

Prescribed to be represented at the initial launch.
A ship flying unknown colors is boarded
With the extraneous material
From what they used to build it
For its cargo. Mere forgetfulness cannot remove it.
It must be delivered like a stowaway plant
Channeled from what was an ocean
You proclaimed real. Sight once
Met its invisible maker, never to be known
As being capable of even looking, except
Its gaze still haunted you in the library.
You can't live there. There are the attacks
On all veiled keeping of things
In one place, hidden from existence
Like existence is from itself. The event
Didn't happen until they left it
Alone in this vast medium. One often finds
The thing you've started out to say's
Been passed as through a factory of children
Whispering one phrase from one person to the next,
The single iron bolt of thought moved through a forge
And the final product nowhere in peripheral sight
But directly before you. This
"Not-being-us" is all that's been hoped
To be portrayed, and you are allowing its art in,
Though it is unlike us, except that it too

Knows nothing that hasn't been adjusted
To include its shadow and this bent curve.
There are principles in art that interrupt you
At the moment of saying that. This gone thing
Is here now: the painter's
Transfixed gaze on you that tells you to look.
The floral seductress grows its wild
Frontier, and he must be secretly pleased
To have had little to do with fertility
As a means of communication, except to throw
Its reception, so as to create something new,
Uncertain of the proof, widely available
But an unordinary image that placates whatever
Comes to it to be included therein.
One of those things lingering in its otherness
Clouds the crystal, and one is what no one
Can say is guaranteed to apparate.
The thought-associations have grown seasonal
And thus limited by nature, and it is
In those that the reflection can't tell
One frequency from another. He has stockpiled
The logicians and made them sing
To the tragedian, and he in turn has seen
The moment of a sphere placed in its room
Which is its sphere returned to a life
Pressed to the right angles our human faculty

Self-Portrait in a Convex Mirror 2

Can understand as one can know that flight
Is a form of work. Our productions
Are forced to read into their purpose:
To see the designer on his stoop
Approaching the implications of a hat—
Which is to say someone put it there.
To be serious about light in the desert
Is one way of being serious. The metallic
Ring receives its viewers, apocalyptically,
Near peak, too close to intervene.
But the remains where the eye can take in
Gold, green, and blue left on the panel
Like something you might step in
Do remain, alternately seen, acknowledged,
Left in place, barely touched by being named.
It is the mental structure that's history,
And that's been moved. Each of these refined persons
Has lost his assignation, outside of matter,
Presented as that which we've been inside
All along, rich with what was given
To help us, whatever the situation may be.
Yes, I know that taste is a matter
Of itself and is placed in the room with the same
Inevitability as furniture. Civilization suggests
One adjust within reason to the exhausted world,
The point being awkwardly folded. Our first steps

Seek refuge in the possibility
Of return. Aping a former world
Might be the next best means of being
There, but one minds the change in scale
As much as one minds the weather when indoors,
Which is to say entirely. Francesco:
There is only one bullet in the chamber:
One looking at you from the wrong end
Of a telescope as you fall back
At a speed that suggests its own potential
As if accomplished by the growth of this
"It was all a dream" syndrome. Though all
Is to be included here, we are quickly
Given back to our reason for developing a preference
To the concrete world—that we left it being
Our temporary accomplishment. The source they are
Is giving up. The convention materializes from its own
Stupor. Push forward, forsaking a naïveté
And all the other silent alarms
Which are telling you, in this straw-colored space,
To exit the room, walk away from the mirror and be
Forever escaping one thing for the next,
In circulation, the waterwheel collecting in
An imitative land, though one which is
Constantly refreshed. The underground
Is organized around a more austere notion

Self-Portrait in a Convex Mirror 2

Of life that has to do with the penultimate
And is less defined by the present,
That old standard, than by the separation of it
From what's about to crest into
Memory's gallery, where you look at yourself twice.
You can't live there. Though on the surface of it
There seems no direct reason why not
To go on being imagined by the portrait's will,
For the net is drawn tight; each sacred place
Remembers others. It seemed meaningful
That some felt this way in their urban setting,
Branching outward into dissolution as does
The fact that breath is normal
And permits no answer. One stocks
Metaphor like the staple of an ideal world
In which nothing shows itself permanently
Like said One. Somewhere a sign makes itself.
Somewhere you can live as childlessly
As the candid sky, but you knew that
Already, and still you looked to renew
The feeling via this well of finished
Observations, vaguely asking the menace
What exactly were the intentions behind
Unlocking this gate if it were not just
To exercise one tactic which was all along
Just to make a decision, any one

Based on a conviction as specific as instinct.
Tread lightly, comrade, the volume
Has increased, and every noise might give you away.
You sense the empty spaces behind the closet doors,
Not to mention the tapestry, which cannot be
Pulled away to reveal its hidden recesses
No one knew of. Our faces revolve
Like ethereal globes that know nothing,
Though they look at you, persistently.
Confront the shades before it's too late
To remember their undeveloped language
And be forced instead to accommodate them
When they arrive at the folding door
To inclusion. What was not meant as exile
Soon became that, as Italy becomes a surface
That cannot be lifted. The popular example
Of "form as meaning" emerges to reaffirm
The perpetuity of that of progress "as everything."
We were at work upon a rarer education
When the sculptors evacuated their basements
Disrupting what was one art and was
Enough. Certainly the leisure to indulge
Established pastimes goes unchecked,
But our own hobby that we've made of memory
Produces such doggerel that, despite being
Comprised primarily of ideas, it seeps into the language.

Self-Portrait in a Convex Mirror 2

If there is anything to reign over in this picture,
Its court has long since given way to another
Life-obstructing task whose copy allows it
To appear to us in the form of a complete system
Where one version matters to the other,
And their exchange is so constant as to make them
A collaborative being dictating its life in
The visual sphere. Yet we are such animals
That know no others but ones with human qualities
Like depth and like little outfits sometimes
In this hued world of whatever. This part
Is here now: the painter's
Version of his face reflected back
From what was once more than the idea
Of the fields' collision, and is now
More than that again but differently.
We don't need paintings or poets
Burst from their vegetal pods into the rose
Marble of a hall lit by silver lamps,
Stolen from some pawn-shop to write by,
Producing a useless yammer after the explosion
Has already been made to be occurring
Constantly from this point of wreckage,
Unannounced. You can go a lot further
Than the corners of a bridge,
Though you might get wetter.

There were clothes that hid nothing,
For it is their folded domain that sees beauty
To its natural door. Draw back
Your hand and cease these familiarities
Such that we have known you all this time
As a being seen through the ridged frame
Eroding from its supports. One wind turns
Into the next, aping naturalness
As if the inner calm were not a tyrant
That demands its prominence but rather
A self with whom we'd have liked
To have rekindled the mysterious advances
Which have led us out to this stained tapestry
To add to our collection of string.
The students knew what an image was before
It came to them in this form, and education
Is a sort of scaring off of ghosts
So that they return to such condensation
At the origin, almost visibly, one unit
To be combined with others that don't
Yet exist, and we've experienced this.
Pretty soon, the shield that greets you
Will be removed, and the invitation
To tell "all" won't be, and won't be
Taken up by your drowned counterpart
But by the disguised master of the room

Self-Portrait in a Convex Mirror 2

Herself, this gibbous city speaking low
And keeping that way too. The complete index
Rushes through the gauze to meet its referents
And find them changed and itself
The force behind their metamorphosis into
What light was carried out or some half-light
In this dimming hour's pageant. Our looking
Through the obscured window never troubled it,
Even when you sketched a diagram of the factors
That comprise thought onto it and the patient
On the other side appeared, somewhat flattened
And surprised at your intrusion. Something
Was picked from the options, and it was
Choice itself, barreling out from its nook
That was everything to be flung over the rail.
There is no longer only the first step.
Things happen closer than that, are resumed
Before they can be summed up by the symbol
For truth which is a mirror, and death
Which is the mirrored vessel
It stays in. The town is developed by
Strange attractors and this conducting
Of water over the burnt grounds drought's
Kept in mind that the apostle of this
Waking dream travels over, boatlessly.
Among the features of the room, one drifts

Up to show what it meant by
Taking part in the round-up and shaking
Off all ties to the ultimate speed at which
Thoughts form within the parameters
Of a previous condition. The hand holds
No chalk. There are parts
That come off that are not
The whole but were, here and there,
Of something remembered of time.

Self-Portrait in a Convex Mirror 2

For Joseph Kaplan

Acknowledgments

Many thanks to the editors of the following journals in which some of these poems first appeared:

The Awl: De Imagine Mundi 2

CLOCK: "Voyage in Blue 2," "Absolute Clearance 2"

Epiphany: "Self-Portrait in a Convex Mirror 2"

Jubilat: "Farm 2," "Farm II 2," "Farm III 2"

Literati Quarterly: On Autumn Lake 2, Worsening Situation 2, Oleum Misericordiae 2

The The: "River 2"

Gigantic: "Forties Flick 2"

Pinwheel: "City Afternoon 2," "No Way of Knowing 2," "Sand Pail 2," "Robin Hood's Barn 2"